MW00526437

THE NEW WORLD

newer and newer
all the time !

The New World

Kelly Schirmann

Kelly Schirmann

Black Ocean
Boston · Chicago

Black Ocean
P.O. Box 52030
Boston, MA 02205
blackocean.org

Cover Photo & Design by Jay Fiske | jayfiske.space
Book Design by Taylor D. Waring | wanderingreliq.com

Interior Photos by Jay Fiske and Kelly Schirmann

ISBN: 978-1-939568-35-9

Library of Congress Control Number: 2020942730

FIRST EDITION

CONTENTS

for you

ART DURING WARTIME

How do you write poems in a country like this? I asked my friend, a poet. We were at a sunny brunch spot in a gentrifying part of the city. It was one morning of a typical bad-feeling summer—record-breaking temperatures and teenagers dying in police custody. Out the window, people in bright clothes walked back and forth on the sidewalk. I couldn't bear my own identity anymore, which was a person who noticed things and sometimes wrote them down.

I had been under the impression that art should be visionary and instructive—that its most holy function was to transform the soul of the person experiencing it, and that this transformation would lead, eventually, to the improvement of our collective experience on earth. This impression had led me to pursue a life governed by creativity. But say an artist lived, ate, slept, and worked in a country defined by violence and competition—how could they create a vision that reproduced anything else?

In other words, it was a serious question—one I'd asked myself, in recent years, nearly every single day. I imagined my friend would know what I meant—at least about the country. That it was all so brutal and garish and cruel, and that to be complicit in the cruelty, by virtue of your citizenship, was too much to bear. I thought she would agree that the impulse to *be an artist* could no longer be totally trusted, at least without examining what it was you were making, and with whose resources, and why.

My friend had no idea what I was talking about. She frowned and gently touched my wrist. *Art has never been more important,* she said, over our just-arriving breakfasts. What the world needed from me, now more than ever, was to *continue doing my work.* My friend nodded, sure of herself, and began to eat. I stirred my coffee feeling scolded—a woman who thought naively that art emerged when it wanted to, from the body and its energies, like flowers from dirt.

I knew my friend didn't really mean *me* or *my work*—she meant all poets, and whatever work it was they did. She meant anyone who could look upon some half-lit garbage, or a series of weird photographs, and say, with some confidence: *this is a poem.* I knew that what she wanted was to pretend, momentarily, that we lived in a world in which the validity of art and art-making was never questioned. I wanted the same world, I guess, but no longer knew if we could afford it.

I had no idea who would understand this. My friend wore an expensive blouse and she smelled like rosewater and behind her the sky was hazed with smoke from the wildfires, portentous and beautiful. She was telling me her belief system, which was that artists should continue working even though the world had ceased to. This was a seductive idea, as it eliminated all other options—I *had* to. But how?

How is not *why*, though I could have asked that question, too. Why write at all, if afterward I still felt helpless to escape my debts, or fell asleep thinking of our nuclear oceans? Why write if it was not softening me to the imperfections of others, or purifying my soul through intentional action? And what if, by writing from a place of fear and despair and cynicism, I made others feel afraid, or desperate, or cynical?

I didn't ask this. My friend and I ate smoked trout in a window booth, and the conversation moved toward the things in our lives that we could see: our work and partners and exercise habits. We did not return to my question, which wasn't a question at all, really: just one of thousands of slivering fears, resisting analysis or burial, but nonetheless always there.

*

How do you make art in a country that's always at war? Maybe this was my real question. Picasso painted such beautiful doves, and still we send human beings into the desert to blow up buildings. All my life I've been told that art is revolutionary, but I still don't know what this means. I can see how it comforts; how generously it distracts. But no novel has convinced a billionaire to pay their taxes. No poem has persuaded our president to end a war.

When I was sixteen, I watched a famous Vietnam movie at a friend's house: half a dozen young soldiers floating a muddy river, smoking joints and reading letters from back home. One by one they die from enemy fire, set to a soundtrack of rock n' roll. Critics refer to it as one of the most powerful anti-war films ever made, despite the fact that the director set hundreds of acres of forest on fire to make it. *My film is not about Vietnam,* he later claimed—*it is Vietnam.* The movie made $150 million at the box office.

Art cannot exist to decorate an intrinsically violent society—I wrote this in a different poem, years ago. At the time I lived in a city where long-time residents were being aggressively displaced, and where muralists were being hired to paint uplifting phrases on the sides of expensive new grocery stores. *Keep your head up!* they encouraged. Tourists took photos in front of them, holding gourmet ice cream cones and flashing the symbol for peace.

I do admire the impulse to add beauty to the world, or to offer some respite to others as they navigate the specific difficulty of being alive. When I feel helpless or stuck, words and songs are what move me forward. But I wonder at the function of art in an age of empire, when it might be more useful to hold the gaze of our reflection a little longer. What would it look like to confront the reality and pain of the aggressive displacement, for example, instead of escaping into the momentary distraction of paint?

Escapism is necessary, of course, if we want to survive the present, or hold out hope for a little change. The line is so thin, though, between optimism and complacency. After the election, one of the ways we consoled ourselves was by insisting that *art would be great* under fascism; like punk music in the 80s, or all those films about World War II. The quality of art would increase, we argued, even as the quality of life for humans everywhere declined. The consumer product held up (here) as a justification for human suffering (there). How else do we explain capitalism, if not that?

It's true that art has never been more available—that in an effort to make meaning of our ongoing political disasters we continue to produce more and more. The streams are saturated now with photos and fragments—news of developing products, reminders of older products for sale. The production is undertaken with a sense of urgency, like in any wartime economy. All of it together creates a more beautiful tunnel through which massive streams of corporate capital flow.

And so producing art is a challenge if you want to make a different world. There is no way to trust that the famous magazines, the ones we all want to be published in, are not using our feelings to humanize their war. Even a revolutionary poem, when painted on the side of a tank, can be usurped for empire. Even still, we have to eat—and more than that, we want to feel we exist. We put our poem on the tank and watch the tank roll through the streets. We hope, somehow, that something good will come of it.

Despite all this, I get the sense that the artists of this country believe their creative endeavors—by their very nature—are in intrinsic opposition to the network of violence and profit and political corruption that our country represents. I don't think they are. In fact, I think it's entirely possible that the art we are producing—consumer objects, entertainment, interior decoration—is perfectly compliant with empire. That most of what we are making isn't revolutionary at all.

Earlier this spring, I watched a video clip of fifty-eight missiles being launched at a Syrian Air Force base. The network news anchor narrating the live footage was so moved by the sight of weaponry, by the possibilities these weapons presented for him, that he quoted the late poet Leonard Cohen on the air. *I am guided by the beauty of our weapons,* he breathed. His eyes lit up like a child's. On the screen behind him, a massive military arsenal sailed through the air in the dark, en route to inevitable deployment in a country already devastated by bombs.

Art can be enlisted, I thought, and I noticed that this was happening all the time. Painters are hired to design sweatshop sneakers, and writers are paid to humanize political speeches, and all of us visit daily the translucent digital hubs where we publish content for free, all in the service of state surveillance and corporate revenue. Art, regrettably, is just one way to soften the horrors of war without ever having to change the system that perpetuates them. I watch the artists of our country fit themselves to the supply chain, preoccupied with the desire to be told, at last, that they have worth.

*

The sky is a hot bright blue. I'm in another city, eating another breakfast, and listening to a different friend tell me about a woman who works at a fulfillment center for a massive online retailer. This woman is one worker on an assembly line comprised of hundreds of people. Her job is to fill boxes with retail products, seal them, and send them further down the line to be shipped. Her human labor, unending and unbroken, is what makes the products go down the line as quickly as possible. Her speed and focus results in more profits for the company—regardless of this, of course, her wages do not change.

The woman on the assembly line begins to feel bad one day. She tells those on the line next to her that she thinks he is having a heart attack. In fact, she collapses shortly after she says this. The assembly line managers, who know that the entire purpose of the line and its quickness are to increase the company's profits, do not stop the line to help this woman. Instead the line continues, and her co-workers are urged to keep going, despite the terror of working alongside someone who may be dying, or dead.

The thing about endurance is that we can only endure so much. Most days I walk in circles around my house, or perform monologues to empty rooms, or drag thoughts around on paper in an effort to recreate the ways in which my mind once bent. All around me as rents rise and more people give birth, other artists insist that I, an artist, need not be deterred—that despite these things, or in performed defiance of them, what they and the world need most from me, *now more than ever*, is my continued creative production.

But I am often sad about the world, and tired from living in it. Those who would ask me to produce beauty do not live in my body, do not feel its efforts and limitations and desire for rest. I fear that, like my country, they care less about the exhaustion of a body than about the body's capacity to be productive. What could any body offer that would be of value, stooped over on the line like this, churning out half-reactions to thoughts that don't even originate from inside it?

I will tell you this: we all know when art has value, real value, and we all know when it was made out of the belief that an artist must constantly produce. One of these reminds us that war exists, but is separate from humanity, and can be transcended through collective action. The other is an extension of the threat that war presents—that we are nothing beyond our capacity to keep the line moving. That we have no other choice.

The line does not stop, and because of this the body collapses. The line cannot stop and because of its not-stopping the products continue down the line quickly, and the bodies are swept away, and the profit stream is undeterred—the whole thing makes money. The collapsing on the line occurs frequently, and the not-stopping of the line for the collapsed body signifies to the other bodies on the line that the line and its movement are more important than the bodies—that it keeps on going without them, despite them. That there are more bodies available, right behind you, if yours should fail.

The line undeterred and not-stopping is not at all like life, though it is tempting for those on the line to draw the conclusion that it must be. Actual life is not anything—not a program or a ladder or a series of rules. It is an experience that is stopped often, interrupted and redirected constantly. It is during these moments of interruption, when the cool air rushes in, when we are most susceptible to art's arrival—to allowing ourselves to be transformed. The line is separate from us, and its continuation is not our own. We owe it nothing.

We could rest.

*

Before the world became what it is now, a scatter of narratives funneling (corralled) toward the One Story, my mind was a house with infinite rooms. Then the world became an emergency, and the sirens were so loud, and our crises were projected onto the tallest buildings, beneath which people gathered daily to exchange notes and re-enact their fears.

The implication was that everyone should fixate their entire attention upon the One Story, in all its entropy, which resulted in every artist leaving their post to watch and describe the spectacle of war.

I wanted to participate, having no other ideas. I was angry, like the others, and so I practiced being attentive. I made my body porous and sharp like lava rock, meant for scraping skin. I abandoned beauty, seeing so little of it, and I let the world and the Story and all kinds of things pass through and into me. I wrote down what I noticed, which was, I believed, the main responsibility of a poet.

I noticed weather patterns, severe dreams, cruel and stupid men, the rampant abuse of language, the arbitrary games of money, embedded messages (flags and pop songs), our accumulated waste, our campaigns for nostalgia, the sudden popularity of astrology, another new shop for curated art objects, class warfare, what could calm me down, how gun conversations went, how the eclipse moved us, briefly, and then how there were just three channels left—how all the parks had been dug up in the middle of the night.

I did not feel victorious, noticing this. I cried and slept and wore blood-colored clothing and walked alone and with others and talked around these things, little jagged curios in the street, whose awful shapes trailed behind me, existing as proof that I was alive, and myself, and paying attention.

This is what I want to say: that I walked and collapsed and threw things and felt ashamed, that still I could only be who I was, and so I wrote it all down selfishly, hoping that one day we could talk.

How do you make art during wartime? You make it for everyone living, everyone hoping that it will change. You stop often, and are so careful, that your mind not be a gun or an assembly line. That it be anything but a vision of a world that isn't here yet— one you have to believe will be here soon.

THE NEW WORLD

We cross through to California at sundown, when the checkpoints are all closed, bringing no fruit or invasive plants, ashing our joints discreetly out the window. We slip past the lit gates unceremoniously, relieved to have not interacted with a man in uniform, to have not needed to think of something to say. We wind slowly through the woods corridor, watching close for chunks of fallen rock on the highway or the glow-white eyes of deer. Only the public radio tones are going, low and frantic like insects on a lake, the buzz of it all descending, the knowledge that the world has changed. An old sign welcomes us in and I see it at once as an artifact, see how it will be unearthed one day, caked mud covering the bullet holes and state flowers. *How kind we'll all seem*, I think. We pass into the dark newness, ready to become something else.

We want evidence, I guess, that the world is not cruel. Jay takes the highway stretches going ten under the speed limit. He waves to the other cars to pass us by. The city trickles into beige shopping centers, then rest stops, then trees. The sky is a pale blue: I believe that my life is now mine. I think of the people we're leaving saying *change is inevitable!*—meaning the forever construction of luxury apartments, the grating and filling of empty fields. But when this new road unribbons I feel that lakewater feeling of getting out from under it, of erasing the old world entirely. I feel that it's gone—how simple it really is to *go*. Outside the sky hazes downward into a deep gold, then further to the hard white of sun: the non-color of pure heat. I put my hands out the window, into the cool wind, where information scatters like pollen, giving birth to something grandiose.

When you need a new world, it's because the old world is no longer enough. It's because the old world, as you've arranged it, is trying to kill you. We push along the dark highway away from it, all our possessions in polyester bags. The world I've arranged is a city being colonized by ad revenue. Or it is a belief system made schizophrenic by network news. Or it is just me, alone in my mind, sifting through images of potential shapes for my life, none of which entirely fit, watching my peers grow older on various screens. The shimmer of this world fatigues me, heavies me. Outside, in the tangible world, the sky is changing. Arriving elsewhere, incrementally, I begin to believe it can be left behind.

Our new world is empty, or empty enough, and we know nothing, but are certain our souls will flourish here. Knowing nothing and being certain—a pleasurable, American feeling. We stand in the parking lot of a grocery store and take stock. Marshland, wet with fog, big and flat with far-flung horizons. Glass on watery glass and evergreen hills. It's a not-known California, a gray and misting one, a poor and desolate one, whatever we can afford. Still—the whole state shares the same ocean, the same past, shares the hungry air of gold rush acid freaks and streams of silver money, of speculation and dreams of speculation stitched in astral threads. *All this space*, we think. The fog stinks like weed and sits heavy with money, with the thick American past—what we all share. It's fragrant and bitter. It's been waiting just for us.

I begin to pay attention to signs and symbols, warming to my intuition that we arrived here by some grand design. When we take a walk in our new neighborhood Jay says, *We've been here before.* He points to a muddied horse: *Do I remember?* I write this down. We live on a spit of land between the bay and the ocean, composed almost entirely of sand dunes. *Shifting*, I note. I feel nervous and special. The ocean is gray and grassy—we can hear it churning, on clear days, from our bed. The bay is at its most beautiful during low tide, when the stink of mud and sulfur hangs in the fog, and the mud-smooth wetland topography leaves little round pools of sky-colored water in gathers and trails across its expanse, like planets. *An omen*, I note, to be surrounded by water. To allow yourself to be pulled by whatever makes its waves.

There are blueberry bushes in the front yard, thick and shrubby, rooted through their barrels. They fruit for months. The landlords live around the corner, a loveless couple who drop by most mornings to check on the cannabis plants they keep in the garage. Otherwise, they're indifferent to us, which calms me—my vision of our house is a fortress through which no world can enter. With the ease and comfort of a barrier in place, I allow myself to arrive inside my body. I sleep late for the first time in years, half-waking and repositioning and then diving back into sleep for hours each morning. I dream languid, pleasurable dreams—an orangey respite from the dry world outside. Here on earth, and yet not. I begin to prefer to be alive this way. I suck on my dreams like watermelon candy.

Predictably, I feel energized by our new world. I recall our old world as having become an inevitable gift shop of itself. I think of it with a slow-blooming tenderness that surprises me. This new world, in contrast, is still just ideas—they sear white-hot into my imagination, inviting my critique. I buy a paper cup of coffee and walk through town, communing with my new skin. I heft a jade plant at the nursery, admiring how superstitiously it sits in its pot. *A good luck plant*, the woman at the counter offers, which nearly makes me lose my nerve. Luck is a bright-red word: too obvious. What I want is to aerate my soul-dirt from years of hydraulic stomping. *It's for my soul-dirt*, I tell her, counting out change. The woman doesn't look at me. She slides my receipt across the counter and tells me to have a nice day.

In the morning, I write a list in my notebook, like a permanent to-do: *Eat Air, Move Upward, Go Slow*. I have no idea what this list means, though it glows with the power of someone who does. Just looking at it, I feel myself solidify, and just feeling myself solidify, I wonder where I am in relation to me, or who I'll eventually become. I begin to make more lists. I buy a box of felt-tip markers and experiment with different colors, making drawings and diagrams alongside the lists in pinks and oranges and teals. I draw charts and graphs with more and more confidence, and I label them things like *Shape of Infinite-Story Narratives* and *Military Funding vs. Popularity ($) of Art Form*. The drawings are whimsical and bright. Flipping quickly through these pages, it is almost possible to miss what they are trying to tell me.

Days are silken and healing. When Jay comes home I remember I am part of the world, and I show him my drawings, and he agrees that they are important. We walk to the dunes barefoot, through the scratching overgrown juniper, watching out for broken bottles or sleeping bodies along the trail. Jay takes photographs of the dune grass being shaken by wind, the gray and heavy sand. No one's out there. It's easy to think that we've died, either just the two of us or the whole world, and both feel possible: almost sweet. The year drains slowly into the next one, the future made real by ritual, or pure belief. When winter descends, inevitably, on the panicked world, the rain falls calm and miserable. It drowns out the distant pop of firearms from the shooting range, which has become, to us, its own kind of ambience.

On our dune I feel untethered: part of no world I've been shown. The grey sea mists upward into fog, difficult to photograph, which brings me relief—I can walk alongside it knowing it's just us. Mornings I unfold myself carefully, notice where I'm creased, shake me out briskly, then resolve to fold another way. I feel language leave me, time pass, contentment. My body thickens with light. When the weak sun burns through the midday haze the sky un-pieces, revealing its immensity, and then I see where I am. Beneath this disk of sky I sleep and walk alongside others sleeping and walking. To think of the world this way calms me. I can forget, briefly, why I ever wanted to leave.

I drive my body into town, some days, just to watch it moving through the world. This tells me how far I am from what I want, which is to exist with grace and levity within a country I don't understand. I buy a coffee at the grocery store and then scan the newspapers, allowing myself a brief window within which to feel anger or despair. The headlines are similar and urgent: they spiral around each other in a frenzy, wanting me to believe the world has broken in half. At first glance, I can see how ridiculous this is. When I pick them up, though, I'm not so sure. Standing there a little longer, I begin to pulse alongside them. They hold two broken pieces in front of me, shaking and desperate. *Before and After*, they say. *Old and New*.

I pulse around town for a while, trying to walk my body back to sand. The sidewalks are empty, the pastel storefronts bleached by sky. I don't like the theory of a broken world, which suggests that without devastating loss, the world cannot be remade. I don't like the idea that nothing can be new without discarding what it has been, or is; or that the world becomes new all at once, for everyone, based on a single tragedy. Back home, I try to remember that time is ancient and continuous, like the ocean—that every newness isn't actually brand new, but the product of a long line of decisions that has led, inevitably, to now. That this now-ness, even, will become then-ness so quickly: that this is the way things are. Still, it's hard to stop my mind from repeating the wrong thoughts it is given. If I forget to think, or walk, I give in. I let my mind break time into two pieces. *That was the old world*, it thinks, *and this is the new one*.

I begin to feel the new world seeping into my thoughts. On my grey beach each morning its language pricks and frazzles me, scattering the birds before I can really see them. I feel resentful, then deflated by the existence of resentment within me, and then walk the long trail home with wet boots, a little lost. How is a person supposed to understand the new world, and their place in it, when it inserts itself without their permission, before they can really even make up their mind? It arrives with no memory, and cuts out so much—books and films we haven't understood yet, architecture that doesn't make us sick. But people are hungry for newness, however it comes. I make a hot bath and shake lemon oil into it, feeling an elusive clarity ebb away from me again.

All of my rituals begin to feel stale. I make the drive into town most mornings to buy a coffee at the grocery store and look at all the headlines. I know I shouldn't get involved with such garish narratives, but how else will I commune with the world, or even know what it is? With its hooks in me, I feel powerless and connected. I heft the newsprint, skim its bad news, then wander the aisles, dejected. I finger the bamboo kitchen tools and sea salt toothpastes absently, wanting to believe that these objects represent something meaningful. Then I play a game with myself on the way out of the store, where the first thing I see will be a metaphor for the whole universe. Sometimes it's a mother helping her children navigate the busy parking lot. Other times it's a person sitting alone in the driver's seat, staring at a screen.

I decide to study newness like a person, or stars. I write down what I notice, which is all I can really do. We are intoxicated, it seems, with the knowledge that the world can change—even a terrifying change is a symbol of something new, and therefore exciting. Though the newness of the world does terrify us, it also explains away our despair, which can now be blamed on those who made it change and not the history that preceded it. I heat soup and eat it slowly, my eyes to the blinding light. I read poems and essays about the new world, look at paintings depicting it, sign petitions to reverse it, donate money to keep it at bay. I watch the men made rich by newness, by clothing and technology and information, fix this language onto our tired history. I watch the rest of us follow along, exhausted. Waking and scrolling, eager to learn what the world is now.

It's all changing, the landlord remarks one morning. He's crouched on the floor of the garage, adjusting the drip irrigation system. He's been listening to a series of popular audio recordings, made by a former game show host, which regularly cite the benefits of psychedelic drug use. This, he believes, is evidence that the world will right itself eventually, or that maybe it already has. The landlord seems to think that information needs to be exploded from our institutions like natural gas—that this information, in the light of day, will create balance. I clutch my bath robe, unsure. When he leaves, I shake lavender oil into the diffuser, watching the dark clouds roll in from the skylight above the bed. *Everything is changing*, I write in my notebook. It reeks of me convincing me, which is the only poem I can manage to write.

It's easy to say why we want new things, and even easier to find out where to get them. By pressing a delicate button on a small device, I can be made aware of every newness the world has to offer. I can identify a new desire, then work to fulfill that desire, and then abandon it for the next one, which is one of the many ways I can pass the time while I am alive on earth. What I want to know is whether I should allow myself to want new things at all, much less to get them, because how long could we all really go on this way—piling our garbage in mounds, leaving one city for the next? When the world is spent, at last, of newness, what will happen then? We'll have no choice but to return to something we've already seen and pretend we've never seen it before.

I fall asleep in my robe, scrolling through images of other women making art. When I wake up an hour later on the couch, the sight of pale blue daylight coming in through the windows falls around me like a shroud. I make coffee and take a drive to the marsh, feeling worried about where it will all go. Our desires, I mean—the objects and futures we think we want, which we won't want for long, and which all have to end up somewhere. In the streams, I've seen a lot of promises—that the next world will be more meaningful, that we won't be the kind of people to dispose of things so quickly. I remember the lakewater feeling of leaving, and wish I could feel it again, and am ashamed. I take the long loop trail away from the highway, sulking, and watch the herons stalk around for fish.

Winter rounds in an arc toward spring: swathes of bleated grass dry out, rankle, and stretch skyward. Outside the grocery store I lean against the stucco, absorbing the sun's weak pulse. *I'm so tired*, I write, then watch the pigeons, unable to think of anything else. Earlier I'd rubbed eucalyptus oil on my wrists and neck because I'd started to regret coming to this place, thinking I could escape or outrun the world, or carve a smaller one inside its wreckage. I go inside and buy a cup of coffee, shuffle over to the headlines again. The newness is getting old, losing its grip—you can smell it in the aisles, like overripe fruit. I watch the people pass by, hefting their vegetables, ignoring the news altogether. I get a curious thrill noticing this. I see the story of the new world lift slightly from the world itself, suspended there above its crust, just briefly, like fog.

I wake to pale blue in the skylight, feeling resolved to change. *The work of the artist is to refuse imposition*, I write, remembering that the world is my subject, not the other way around. I skim an article about the most recent developments in a billionaire's mission to colonize Mars, practicing interpreting reality for myself. The Mars mission has been undertaken, as far as I can tell, because our collective inability to regulate our economic system has overheated an entire planet. Despite his confidence, I get the impression that the billionaire is lonely and has run out of ideas. It makes me wonder if newness is always the consolation of loss. I write in my notebook, *newness is always the consolation of loss*. It's so easy, I note, to make a truth out of a fascination. I remind myself that this is what is happening all around me, all over the world, all the time.

When Jay comes home, I tell him about my plan. He approves, reminding me that I can seek out existing solutions instead of trying to invent my own. I fall asleep on his chest. In the morning, I wash my hair with apple cider vinegar, listening to the rain fall on the skylight. I play an audio recording of two men discussing the use of mushrooms in cleaning up superfund sites. Apparently fungal cultures, once inoculated, can process and dispose of heavy metals—they have the potential to filter thousands of acres of coastline that humans have contaminated with oil spills. I discover, while listening, that I somehow already know this. Another man interrupts. *Who is going to pay for that?* he wants to know.

My return to the world is slow going. I practice believing I can absorb information without feeling panic or rage. I begin to imagine the new world as suffering from a crisis of narrative—if I can create a story about what it is, I think, I can make it whole again, and then find myself inside of it. This prospect is thrilling: blood flowering into a dead limb. I return to my notes with a newfound energy, eager to learn what everything means.

Money is the stick we're beaten with, I'd written, in slanting letters with rich green ink. I read it again, frowning, unsure of what it says. In the pages that follow I'd drawn diagrams of how language worked; extensive notes for a book about walking; field sketches of various clouds. I hunt a while for something cohesive, then pile the notebooks in the kitchen, depressed. The landlord is putzing around outside, humming loudly, banging the hoses against the deck. I think about going to say hello but I'm already caught in the house, reading an article about the Mars billionaire, who says he will give out free flamethrowers to anyone who attends the release of one of his new cars.

I feel too porous to read, and too empty to write. In bed, I picture my whole body as a sea sponge—foamy and yielding, with big soft holes. I get angry with myself because this is not how a poet should be. A poet is emotional, yes, but rigid, too—they make their mess within a form, which is the only way people can stand them. I don't know any forms and am drained of my feelings just from being alive. Still, supposedly, I want to be an artist. I eat buttered toast at the coffee table, thinking this over. When a tree is too slow to fruit, scientists invent new trees with quicker apples. This thought makes me scared, and emptier still. *Who are the scientists?* I wonder. What did a quick apple taste like?

When Jay comes home I'm back in bed. My eyes are puffy with tears, because I am a tree farm of a person, which everyone knows is bad for the world. I want to believe that newness can exist, and this has put big holes on the earth, and inside me, and now neither of us will ever be whole again. He makes me apples with peanut butter and then takes me outside, where the sun is shining on the fat tips of aloe plants. There are no holes in any of it, at least not big enough to crawl or fall into. This gives me a little courage. *The earth doesn't need us,* he says, and I know what he means, and the dark weight of me slips beneath the surface, falling down joyfully toward some hidden and meaningful stream.

Fruit season is coming around slow. We buy cups of fresh vegetable juice from the grocery store and walk the empty streets of town, the dark purple stain of beets turning the corners of our mouth upward, and red. People drive by in their cars, stomped-on seeming. They edge us out of the crosswalks, chopping the air with their palms. It makes me angry, but it's also a chance to practice. I begin to invent different ways of looking at them, looking way deep in there, through their fogged-in little windshields, into their actual faces. The purpose of these looks is to touch them, to remind them that we both exist. One of the looks says, *What the fuck is your problem, asshole?* Another one says, *I'm sorry you don't have anyone to help you destroy your pain.*

That night I dream I'm walking down rough stone streets, along a row of identical houses. I stop at the last one and open the door. Crowding the threshold are plants: big leafy green plants, succulents and cacti and jungle palms. I greet them, excited and curious. As I reach forward, I notice my left hand is gloved in a thin brown cotton. I spread my fingers to examine it—*Like leggings*, I think. When I wake up from my plant dream I feel touched and whole, like I've been visited by a dead relative. I've never been contacted by plants before, and I want to be methodical and respectful about interpreting their messages. I search *significance of gloved left hand in dreams*, hoping this will bring me closer. My search returns several pages for dream guides, each ranked in the contemporary five-star system, with links to purchase them online.

No one understands what dreams are, I write. This excites me—I have a reason, now, to keep trying. Spring is coming: the sun weak and promising. I sit on a bench near the bakery, watching the wind blow leaves and cigarettes around my feet. Nobody understands dreams, and still we have them—still we let them exist in and alongside us, always welcoming more. I try to leave my thoughts about newness behind, all the baggage of objects and profit. I try to think of a dream like the bay, filling and emptying mysteriously, having nothing to do with me. Watching it breathe there, in my mind, I understand. *The dream is what we are waiting for*, I write. I stand to leave, walking along the breathing bay, feeling all of us curling toward some golden culmination, moving in our own slow arcs around the only sun we have.

I begin to see the world as a place—a sphere of land and water, full of people who are desperate for a new dream. The difficulty of achieving this dream, of course, is almost unbearable—new people arrive every day, knowing nothing, and how can it all be explained? To remove the edge from our desire, we bring new things home with us—little avatars of the future world we dream of. When we remember that these are objects, and not dreams, we dispose of them quickly, ashamed. Slowly, we move forward toward the new world—a system of actions and consequences, not just a series of objects. Every day, we become smarter. We learn to differentiate between what is real and what is pretending to be.

Walking in the world, among its people and buildings, becomes much easier. When big trucks leer six feet behind me, pushing 70 on an old farm road, I think, *this person is desperate for a new dream.* When I see a man and woman and their adolescent son seated at the Thai restaurant, waiting for their food, not speaking to one another, each absorbed by their own screen, I think, *these people are desperate for a new dream.* When I find needles and torn plastic bags along the dunes trail, piles of trash someone has left behind, I pick up what I can. *We are desperate for a new dream,* I think, while watching a movie about discovering life on another planet, which we have barely managed to do on this one.

The moon is full, or close to it, and we put on sweaters and walk out into the dunes. The sun is setting and we take the southern trail onto the high ridge, which overlooks a big sand bowl—a nice viewpoint from which to film the grass and water, and what the wind does to each one. I cried dry tears in the bath earlier, reading my political magazine, but then we'd talked about planting a lavender garden—lavender only—when the weather got better. I tell Jay my ideas about dreams and the world, and he agrees. He says that's what he's waiting for, too. He sets the camera up on the ridge and we sit for a while, thinking. Clean, windy moon air shushes my cheeks. We let it go until the sky drains itself, then turn it off and walk home.

I wake beneath the pale skylight feeling energized. I shower and dress and wash the sheets. I open the doors and windows, letting the wind blow my notes around. *The new world is a place*, I write, and circle this sentence with turquoise ink. I add orange lines stretching outward to denote a sun. I am happy with this development. Outside, the sky breaks and curdles like milk, the breeze breathing the whole thing blue. I make coffee and eat two clementines, listening to the landlord humming from the kitchen window. It's a nice song, plain and sweet. I drink my coffee and watch her for a while, stooped over in the sandy yard, cutting away the yellowed chunks of old shrub.

THE DREAMS

DREAM OF TAKING NOTES

I dreamed a long hallway
made of language

There was a hard white sky
that backlit the fluorescent
grass and there was my body
That's what I remember

In the morning I forget
to write down where I've been

If I obliterate me
in the stream it's worse

These past few years I've watched us
slack a little from our frames

Like wood left out
through the seasons

Held by thin nails

Tiny death lessons

Where is my thing to say
In my dream the world collapses
into the season I noticed
the shaking of leaves in wind
& drove with blue thoughts
down empty roads luxuriously

Growing larger / like vapor
Never repeating myself

Some nights I cry
thinking I've used my softness
up / with so much time to go

What stops me
from being me again

Notifications

A good thought
passing by me
in its boat

DREAM OF GOODBYE

I can't leave this
plane or grid behind

Mind hangs up like
silk scarf in winter bush

Photogenic

I dreamed I gave up
trying to say anything real in a poem

Fragmentation is what's real
I mentioned this

at breakfast / when you slid
coffee into a thermos for me

Frowned at that word

Leaving is real
when you pull up for gas in Eastern WA
and your dog whines and licks

A cold wind sweeping
through abandoned orchards

I was waving

Goodbye
West Coast

Fruitful and starving

to unshelve your clay ranges
and sink into the ocean at last

DREAM OF A NEW WORLD

I got grass marks on my belly
dreaming a long luxurious dream

I was the well I dug out of me
for the whole world to drink from
and woke to an orange wind

I said I wouldn't put a freeway in a poem
but someone put several of them
through my life

In my sleep

We walked as far as we could
through the residential blocks

Away from bridges and too-empty
parking lots or strip malls

It was easy to admit
that lots of places make me feel awful

When I'm awake

People like to tell me
I overthink things

or laugh hard at the fruit I picked
thinking I must own acres of it

That I climb those trees for fun

I don't tell just anyone
about the time I died
in that yurt in Southern Oregon

Or that life is too long
for me to miss everyone properly

They are so full and tired
and they never listen

I want to understand

How we can all wake up
on Earth

when so few of us
are actually here

THE NEW WORLD

The New World arrived
when we were unconscious

It laid on top of the Old World
like vellum paper
and showed us what we'd done

There was no one to blame
because everyone was an institution
and therefore subject to rules

There were many new documents
we felt compelled to sign

There was still fresh juice
though we regarded it skeptically

The New World shined
brighter / and was

Red became a color
for the first time in decades

Heat came from humans
who were just pure energy

Food grew faster
and more anonymously

Eventually

The New World split itself
between ideology and action

It made new images
and reproduced them

Many of these images
were of a much Newer World
we hadn't gotten to yet

There was a feeling permeating
all of us / a sleepy memory
of having moved beyond
the moment of choice-making

without having made
a choice at all

The New World for example
was not a singular decision

It was an adjacent performance

Long and slow
Still

I watched it sometimes
when there was nothing else on

Something to clean the house
or prepare food with

Otherwise it was just me

And how quiet it got then

THE NEWS

I dreamed a diverse
group of well-dressed
informants told me *stay here*

It was my favorite room
where I forgot / eventually
to notice the shadows .
of leaves on the porch

Being free now / still
I mold my world to theirs

Every day
I rediscover the benefits
of fresh fruits and vegetables

and wonder if singing is real

There are quite a few convincing theories
as to the fractal nature of the universe

But I don't like the words they use

To wake me up
I force a simple pleasure

I make spare house keys
and keep them on a single ring

At the hardware store exchanging
faces with the others waking
with pleasure I prepare

We prepare as a group
A pleasurable feeling

Prepare for sex for hygiene
for winter / Prepare
to be an artist

I am afraid

In my dream again

I swirl around a new preparation
like leaves in the river

with all of my objects
and think

I want to be useful
and to think useful thoughts

but toward what?

As it is
people act like language
is cake / or an orchid

I know it knows how
to be something else

DREAM OF SYMBOLISM

I get this sketchy feeling about words

Sifting through the newspaper
(that's just an old metaphor)

I want to get away from everyone
but I love it out West

I love Western newness
haunted by the specter
of its own severed ribbon

What's dirtier
The Appalachians are older

They give good hard clay
ready to burn into objects

In the Southwest the dollar stores
are shaped from adobe

Ancient planet history
Swirled into me

A new road cut
into a mountainside
Squabbled over / then
driven over

I want to get away from that
bending feeling

of time arcing & being
in its side car laughing

Giving a little wave

DREAM OF THE FUTURE

Sunsets look different now

It's probably the forest fires
or the way time has striated itself

Before the eclipse came
and went I had thoughts every morning
like *This is the last morning*

or *Theater is so brutish*

Meanwhile everyday

new emotional states

are born and harden
into miniature poisonous
figurines

Orbiting you

Before every stream emptied
into a much saltier ocean

I felt spaceships looking at me
I mean really noticing
Now there's nothing
but the same old hits

And newer and newer hits
aging remarkably

DREAM OF FLAT EARTH

A poem about chimes
is a body entering itself

Information is what
the earth gives me

Naked in the National Forest
Hearing bells in the trees

At the web video
building they're arriving
screaming / *somebody*
see me

Their charts about carbon

God digs deep holes in my brain

I pretend to be interested
in creation myths
when they come up in conversation

Really I'm thinking
of an expensive lifestyle

Like being a painter
or wanting to remember
what the afternoons felt like

on this iteration of the planet
With all the crosswalks razed
& our memories being replaced
by more famous moods

But I was born / I was
a child & then
a kind of sensate
impermanence

& then this blue
blushing sunset midnight forever

Hear me

I do know the way it works:

Language stands closest
to the mind's exit and waits
for a reason to slip out

Like you

it doesn't want to do anything

And like you
it is so desperate
to be tested

DREAM OF A HUNGRY WORLD

Language rings us at different tones

You can say "raiding the commons"
but not "profit = destruction"

if you want to elicit
a brighter color
A pleasing lack of shape

Lots of people write books
angry / edit obliviously

A landscape diminishes
& becomes your blood

My advice for women
is to learn that we are furious

Learn how to get it out

Men grasp
& punch, etc
Women feed their loved ones
anger

A mis-stake / a fence line
made jagged as stars
still works

For now / but

Learn to return again soon

This is a hungry world
full of people

who are always in motion
Always trying to eat

DREAM OF BEING IN AGAIN

I'm in public again
and writing a poem
about the man in a fishing vest
who is watching rap videos

One after another

I'm afraid I'll be disinvited
from many more parties
because I canceled my internet
and I can't control my despair

I'd like to grow cauliflower
successfully / to steam it

to near transparency / to eat it
and absorb all its nutrients

I'm not doing that

Often I feel a strong desire
to drink nothing but water
for several weeks

I'm not doing that either

I understand patterns
I don't understand
needing to understand all of them

There are viral ad campaigns
and then the sentimentality
that pushes them thru

For instance

One evening I noticed
that every dog in the dog park
was lit with a similar LED device

The way a dog runs
at night is different

I think the human demographic
just wanted to see

THE NEW WAR

Mining yourself is exhausting

One human world
emptying completely
into the bigger one
by force

= Making It

I think I could live forever
never talking to anyone

But here we are

My parents are addicted
to conservative news channels
and reality TV programming

I am suspicious of the way
celebrity deaths are mourned

I'm wronging again

Who I love
is a person who remembers basic facts

like how to care for succulents
or where the carburetor is

Me I just get all riled up
watching that old man stir the shit

Just get up on top and stir the shit
like we asked him to

The bag opens endlessly
for my lucrative feelings
to rile up into

Cash register
machine noise

You don't know
how it feels
to be me

HIGHWAY ARCHETYPE

I keep thinking of writing
about what freeways meant
to the folk singers

The truth is I just don't know

To what extent should I be stopped

These are the thoughts of our world
and they are also mine

There are only so many words
So many impulses

There's the highway impulse
& the archetype it reduces to

There's a corn moon
rising yellow over the green sand
I keep thinking

I love poetry & algebra
and they are opposites

One shrinking the other
uselessly / The universe
& what needs to name it

Time bends
& I don't know how

It arcs toward a room service
kind of country
Where all you do is ride

I'm thinking
of a big new road
that isn't new anymore

That anyone can walk along
if they are brave enough

Though I don't really mean "walk"

Though maybe I would have once

DREAM OF WAR & PEACE & WAR

I watched a beautiful expensive film
about Western military prowess

and later I dreamed
such terrible and sexual dreams

Big stabbing bulbs
grown up around an apartment
complex / Theoretically

I've been running to not think
To compact whatever's in the joints
Stop it from fanning out
to the rest of me

Skinned and fat softball elbows

I'd like to never hurt anyone

Peace is a big soft leaf'd thing
Requiring nothing
and therefore confusing

Earlier I fell asleep in the grass
on a warm afternoon

I woke up thinking about money
and a great idea
for a single-topic blog:

People
alone
on their phones
in their parked cars

DREAM OF THE NEW WORLD

There's a big concrete room we gather in
where bad feelings are piped mercilessly

I dreamed I was nightswimming
in the middle of a Russian city
in a warm shallow pool

I put my head under
I thought *Russia is beautiful*

Later I returned
to the type of wet garden fantasy
typical of my socio-economic status

I dreamed my dreams
would cleanse me of what I wanted
to convince others I already had

A working knowledge
of how war is a yin yang

and how to stay full
from sample-sized portions of pasta salads
at corporate health food stores

The sky at night
here in California
is a kind of dead ombre
and I went out under it

I got so high
I wrote a book about walking

Because I think we've forgotten
how to do it

I really think we have

DREAM OF MORE GIRLS

The New World is in danger
of its nectar fermenting

In public spaces everywhere
women are eating figs

They're peeing in the grass
knowing nothing receives
like grass does

and they are right
More are born every day

I don't get scared of the world
but I do get lonely

Waiting here in the dark for them
With the floes of whole years

going by soundlessly
And what will actually change?

Everywhere women
will shoulder the burdens

of wealthy cowards
as they have always done

Drink apple cider vinegar
and gradually lose the ability to maintain
their current data streaming plan

In a dream I carried an angel
but it was a much better word

The new women were arriving
with their smoldering anger

They were extinguishing
their compassion

Dried by the wind

DREAM OF MALLEABILITY

I now believe angels came down to earth
and bleached their own hair
for decades

They stood in a ring of people
and never introduced themselves

My soul gets small

I dumped Epsom salts in the bathtub
as the water came down
hard on the [plastic]

I thought *it's moody here*
and realized I think
I'm moody

Had nothing to contribute
to the message boards

Felt bad about it

Corralled a few scattered terrors
into some art

Ran down the dune
toward the just-set sun
and purpling sky

Sometimes I rotate my life like a mattress

In another version

I watch me imprint my shape into it
Helpless and/or curious
over a period of several years

ADVANCED SYMBOLISM

Hours go by with us
reading old books on African masks

I didn't know Picasso
made so much pottery as he aged
He must have been rich

There's a kind of person
who needs to know you know
what polyrhythms are
and I barely do

In a way
it just means "multiple rhythms"

The lake is frozen over
All of the goats are pregnant

My dad is in Eastern Oregon
videotaping geese

Peaking in the hot tub
later with the radiant snow
I remember who to be

I cry and cry
kneading my pale stomach

Time is a room
you fill with objects
you don't actually want

Earlier I examined
two-dimensional art forms

Later bread soaks up my errant fluids

Then later we trap the sky moving
on an old flash drive

Earlier

the art farm depressed me
The goats / wait no

Later I milk the goats
Later I remember
that oil is so integral
Later
I google the meaning of oil
I don't find much

Earlier was a younger feeling
but I'll have another

Still later
I watch the bright orange
flames raking the air moving
through the woodstove
Earlier
in thick fingers

I do know what makes
music into itself

Really it's just trying

Later
I blow dust from the old masters

Write *Mom* on a piece of paper

Run a line through it

THE NEW WOMEN

Slogans are merciless

They stick in your face like a crease

I believe women have two bodies

One of the bodies knows how
to recognize dissonance

The other body suffers
this dissonance daily

Someone who believes
the past and present belonged
to someone other than females

made a bunch of t-shirts for us

It's a rough game
and nobody likes the rules

The trick is inventing a third body
Graceful and athletic

To send out into the world
and bring back some $$$

THE REVEALING

I found a note I'd written to myself
months or years ago

Let my dad hear my voice more often

Sent him a video of falling snow

Why do I keep forgetting
what it means to be here on earth

When you really grab a hold of it

: saying thank you
: revealing your self

I would be dead
without my friends calling to tell me
their theories about advertisements

I would be dead without music
or poems

(Just play along with me)
(Snow falling on my screen)

Animals are beautiful
and they want your attention

They want you
to make their world better
& I wish I could

I wish I could
have more time on this earth

to become what I could be
and then what I actually am

DREAM OF PEACE

Sitting at a table reserved
for paying customers

wondering who will come out
and shoo me away

Something isn't leaving
Something flew in this morning
Reading about another school shooting

"Reading" = images

Not watching / absorbing pummeling

My scattery capitalised mind
thinking

about mass-producing wallet-sized printouts
of gun violence statistics

to argue with my mom and dad

Weak sun

No one knows

I've spent my whole life
and all of my money
just trying to calm down
and understand what to do

Strong blue sky

All I have are these thoughts
and all my ideas

Poem for banning assault rifles
Poem for living wages

Dry storms that never
coincide with institutional support

Poem for public lands
Poem for walking
then running

What can I never leave my mark on
or what darkens me

Poem for the sky
and strangers

There is a world I know about
but it's not this one
and yet
Poem for the whole world
Poem for not having children
Poem for intimacy
Poem for getting out of the city at last
Poem for the dissolution of borders
Poem for no longer suffering abuse
Poem for peace
Poem for exchange
Poem for silence

POEM FOR HUMOR

I fell apart this year
a million times

A million years ago
I learned how to laugh

then stopped thinking about it
Now walking into mirrors

A darker & darker garden
without a baby

Brush my hair
Put oil in it

Stack of books / here
The songs I like

There's a good boy
pulling it out of me

I learn again

how we all hated growing up
How to forgive the growing

DREAM OF GEOGRAPHY

We were walking through the woods
on a wide path

We were brushing for ticks
That's what you do out here

It was a scrubgrass place
but lush and green

like all of America
It absorbed my projections

that it had been waiting for me
this whole time

I had no need of death
and the spring creek burned my feet

It helped to think of everyone
as an animal

I hoped that none of my desires
would intervene

And thought
I should really thank someone

but so many of my thoughts
are pulled from my mind
almost instantly
like by a wind

APPLES

On our first walk together
I pulled an apple from
a sidewalk tree / Dusted
the chalk of traffic from it
Took a bite
It was premature
It was soured & waxy but
when I offered it to you
you ate & ate
I was performing authority
& sustenance / These bitter
grenades / their hectic juice
Which hurt to hit with
Grow fruit where
they're thrown

Apples are mythic
& obvious / How American
To be named so frivolously
To grow this big
from the wrong word
I dye my clothes
with turmeric because
of climate change / because
of the housing market
I have these too dark
& wet dreams of it
Too warm fruit
squirting / A long arm
chucking it over the fence

But what really changes me
Driving alone & alone
in fields feeling powerless
or pregnant by skimming clouds
The color of the sky / A memory
is a shimmering costume
financed by wage labor
Even so
I felt briefly eternal
gassing up just off some
violent stretch of highway
Elongating my hamstrings
Finding something
timeless to say

Time works on fields
Folds data into dirt
for future memories
Crushed grapes
I wear a straw hat
when I'm unearthing
brown past from brown
soil / Skin is speckling
It's all the same thing
We were talking
close / I felt your arm
meat knowing
this wouldn't last
underground for long
How thrilling
in a topical way
To be engulfed in it
Liked 23k times

Pale geologic wind
blowing to petrification
A man walks the dark
road braced against it
Carrying invasive species
Giving them away as gifts
I watch him diffuse
& bloom into the mist
of a minor celebrity
Everyone loves a freebie
I think / Eating my lunch
in an armored car

Offer fruit
of protection warily
The white flesh is mealy
Has irrelevant taste
Hung a suncatcher
in the kitchen window
as a protest against
weapons
Ate too many apples
today / Wandered
the fields so long

Fruit is preserved
by labor / by suffering
On shelves & web shops
Fruit is preserved
by changing hands
Once an artist walked
through an orchard beholding
the trees for what they were
A lack of hunger
I shrank from her
There isn't time
to hear everyone out

So eating is a problem
Competition narratives
equal culture equal life
where food must be grown
I sleep near open windows
under clean black skies
& I read the book reviews
I check my information
streams / & I wake up
glistening with intention
Ready to participate
in whatever's
on its way

Sure I'm exhausted
& threatened by
color / An avant garde
society filming
the crew of the Mars shuttle
after too much beer
But the distance between
deep knowing & this
kind of smearing
the language present
in my memory
is humor / Wide
like time is wide
but then pithy
& reachable
A joke or
seeds

What grows from all this
It hurts to imagine
Hold something in your pocket
to pass the time / or eat
At school you are given
red apples daily / They shine
like cartoons / Constitute a meal
A visitor came & took us
to the HF / "Hole in Fence"
He pointed / overt
& stupid / Eventually
I hardened into my feeling
A train lugged forward
anciently / I saw me hop it
in my mind

What's ripe today
Traffic chalk souring
ideas of fruit / or fresh ideas
Have seeds will reproduce
You can go buy
forty-fifty acres of trees
though that's generational
Ideas are free now
You peel the stickers
off the skin

What's the word for that
famous expensive plant
I think *trachea* or *endo-*
something / meaning *inside*
Bright green images
encased in your desire
for time to pause
or skip / A little later
I walked to the object store
to find a magazine
to improve my soul
& there it was /
Curated houseplant
Military trouser
Sheer sock
Being an artist

Expression is hunting me
Pastel appropriation / Men
elaborating on sweats
Politic is an aesthetic
OK / I buy enough
of the way others think
I remember he said
that beauty was important
Filled up a stadium
Squeezed plastic
into skin

I'd rather go hungry
Walk myself empty
Milk head propped open
Prepared for release
In the forest a woman
with red hair approached me
You need a clearing
she told me / Stopped
answering my texts

So what clears me
Warm touch & these
little dancings flirted
out outlet-less
Fingers in the paint
I love my beastly
crystalline hopes
for me & the way
I try to fail me less
I love the film
saying women were
multiple women
Permission to
multiply / To think
thoughtless things

Sudden lime green
saturated world
Looks abundant in
the photos / Paints
shadows under eyes
Men gather fuzzing
but less & less now
honestly / Don't feel
for their withdrawal
Feel fear of fear of
taking their place

I practice articulating
what would please me
Crunching apple cream
Fist through the
drywall / No no
this isn't me / The river
flows by / The water
is insincere but briefly
I see peace settling
softly onto the
coming decade
like snow

Yes yes I drink
sometimes the juice
of blooming things
that grow wet leaves in me
That help me sleep
How good of you
when you can to choose
the one that looks the best
& clean it on your shirt
a little / Consider
its power
Give it away

O brief vessel
What is there to
really eat / We have this
little cup of time here
Squeaking red
& slick on the palm
Chainlink fields
& the touching of
circularities
Cough it up
or dismiss yourself
early / Your family
will return to you
First you have to work

Don't remember all I said
Thoughts & thoughts
make heavy the
branches the
world wants me paring
Might as well buy it
Might let it go soft
In my dream
the earth overtakes me
Woke up & went limp
We called it
playing kites

Apple nectar
ferments without trying
Was I grown by
a community or up
from a flung thing
In my egg I could tell
it was relieving / My
expulsion
Some stories last centuries
I wait for my tool
to arrive by mail

Then cut away at something
Then feel the working of
civilizational history
deep into you
We had computers
before / We had
surgical instruments
Throw it out the window
if you don't want to eat it
It isn't littering
It melts in the grass

What keeps me light
Swimming & thinking
alone / with no echoes
of dissonant others
who smudge my priesthood
Who touch my clean ideas
How to guard this but
still belong / How to
guard it all but not think
I need permission
To eat the fruit myself
Eat the flowers
Eat the air

What's ripe today
Need cash infusions
Someone to tell me no
My engine exploded
at the stop light
once / A poet took me home
& now we don't speak
Crunch crunch
Life roughs up the living
Leave me my crystals
My constant secret dark

But what really changes me
Shake thick trunk to let
fall what wants to / What should
Woman with memories
moving swiftly across
the timeline / Child bearing
warbles lessening
Decades keeling into grass

Still no hunger
could make me eat it
National flower
What do I fear
These garish rations
pumped full of identity
Bursting like dog toys
Betraying their seams
I fear a crude world
boiled with talking
& the day our scale models
turn loose of us at last

More now returning
to weeping at folk songs
I see the invisible future
where I'm hooked on
machines / Among the lilac
bushes I wander cold
& freely
I want to change my thinking
about it / Hope only
for crisp pink skin

Hoping to hear
when the globe shifts
finally / I read the poles
switched months or years ago
That the magnet's somewhere new
On the cliffs of this internet
presence I breathe in radiant
sea water / pulsing
My art heroes
soaring above me
Excited to announce
they're rich

What is that
lilting maleness
echoing itself
All the photographs have it
I wish this world went
light on image / Got hungry
for breaking open
I withheld my
triumph narrative
as long as possible
What's power if not that
(Forgetting to photograph
the bright orange snake)

That bright orange apple
is still as radiation
Still something to chew
Lost an hour in the
fluorescent river
Browsing opals
Forgetting my skin
There there / it's soil
that holds me
So nice to
see you in person
A portrait wilting
then giving up

What could I hand over
I only have land
& all this rain
I slide a knife over
the thick part / starving
I'm constantly renewing
You should let me
disappear

Came back to myself
with smelling salts
An infinite ocean
of fitful rest
I mean streaming
content / I mean
bathing on the rocks
Somewhere in the world
is my identity
In my search history
I gulp down green water
Watch the sky ripple
Then sleep

∞

In the morning
I threw a few words on what
the wind was doing
Dried flowers stared at me
& then my mind
was outside making its face

Anyway the world had collapsed
into a swirling pitching
kind of rocking fever
According to songs & films
this was what the world did
often / What the world
might do forever
I was relatively safe on earth
& would have to think this thru

Art is a euphemism
for what we are doing now
Sifting through hills of content
for something symbolic
Of what it all felt like then
Endlessness

Songs & songs coming
one after another endlessly
& easily constructed

Like housing developments
in uninhabited places
Symbolic

Strong wind blows in waves
carving symbols
The ocean scared me
when I lived next to it
Rolling tree trunks in its surf
The rules are easy to understand
& exceptions are always being made
I had parents & I lived somewhere
& this affected my numerology
& credit score / Isn't it feverish
all this cutting in line
at the expense of celestial physics
& our place in it
Anyway

The world was a fine place to begin
noticing things
Just picking them up & holding them
for a while & not getting old
Then time passed & then
it clotted up & unable to flow
through your life it hardened
& your body hardened around it

like the old men who sang those songs
Who sang them a different shape
 I fell in the river & hardened
 in the water / a pleasurable feeling
Knowing I was malleable
& capable of breaking & shift
Wouldn't I exist forever there
Laid out on the warm rocks
Drying my body
or being dried?

Answer me God
I've come all this way
to sift thru the fragments of arguments
in this bold pale future
about our right to what we didn't
none of us make / What someone told us
was made by men

This world
& its naming systems
Its rules & hard fruit
I wake up & need something
to lean against / A hard fruit
to chuck outward from me
To leave seeds & a hand print
No

What I wish
was that we lost this sickness
for being remembered
Was that our books were written
& eaten / Then disappeared

It all hangs there
in the warm air

A poem I wanted to bring you
that could paint a human body
from the inside of this one

I woke up in a fit of longing
to feel the longing of my youth
Old folk song longing
Yellow yellow
longing I felt once & forgot or lost
in the stream of information
In the action of gathering it
daily / I became a woman
& did what my friends said
I said the Big Thing
I said it at parties & stopped
writing back so quickly
& everything fell away
Infinity

is the recognition of this
one arc / this shared story
Circling back to your childhood
& seeing someone else inside it
Walking into a new room
& knowing every room
all the one world & everything in it
returning to you / Everything gold
or fading from it

Violence
& your response to it
& waiting for it to return to you
& knowing what to do

How many cycles are there
Approaching a season
of quietude & visions
I drink clean jars of water
Hope for an opening
in this shared mind
Hope for a newness feeling
The return of light falling down
& in the infinite uncertainty
to hope for a new way
of sitting quietly thru it
To throw prism light

on the wall
Being a person is infinity
Cycling thru that muscular
ever-light / then loneliness
then curling certitude
Full of unspent talk

& to find you again
on the same planet
discarding painful ideas
Addressing the mountain
purpling your skin
I repeat

The world is not new
Was never & couldn't
be new / as a body is barely
new & invents nothing but
strings of words / but
new colors for what we have
been / eternally are
Awake & fearful
or sleeping & dreaming
of fear / Or waking
Anyway
  The world was everything & experience
& I filled it with color & fear

& depression / I walked in it naked
& it was water & my long arms
& I wanted to leave & left it
There were no art grants or rewards
& barely a few open mouths
anymore / No one watching me
collect my groceries in wonder
or lope across the street
I laugh & think
More for me about the world
& this is a scar that works
for now

Do you ever of course you do
discover you groping for a place
to commune in / To be easeful
Don't you want a symbol
that holds you like a room
Most things
you don't need words for
That bright joy of air
& your limbs attached
to the pulse of the unsymbol'd world
& moving alongside it
Wordless in the stream
What am I doing here
on this earth walking & aware

of my legs tiring
Wondering what you want to eat

I heft a book about breathing
written in the middle of
the last century across
the threshold of this new one
& ask for a timeless kind
of thinking / That my body
has the same components
I repeat

Infinity
is reading the same books
& having the same thoughts
in response / Over & over
again / The same lust

& we will need this
desire for circuitousness
when we lose the impulse
to dig back further
into the world we left
before the towers fell
& when the computers failed
to destroy our civilization
Scorched earth histories
we don't dig under

I repeat
I get so lonely
in this world / I get so swollen
in the fluorescent river
A rainbow slowly
poisoning me with images
of the future / I float
sleepily / I repeat

The future isn't anything
A series of decisions
made daily / & right now
To wake up or not
To drag you across
the threshold
Add your name to the list

I'm asking you
Please be in charge
of the coming world
I love your hair
& rapt attention
I love the sun
eating your floor
& I love your tired
& lustful hope
That our bodies radiate

when they detect beauty
I love
Anyway
I hope you live thru it all
There is a going in you
that is your decision
to let go / & how quickly

There is a spherical
feeling we are all making
You can ask it to come
down to you / You can
tell it to leave
You can fix yourself
to the world you are
gracing / just briefly

or try again tomorrow
A good sky lighting you
with color / a goodbye

for which I'm invisible
for which I hold hope for
The handing over
& disappearing & becoming
mere feeling in deference
of offerings / for you
now

For you are the one now
You are the one who
is reading this now

Not me

Kelly Schirmann is from Northern California. She is the author of *Popular Music* (Black Ocean) and the co-author, with Tyler Brewington, of *Boyfriend Mountain* and *Nature Machine* (Poor Claudia). She lives & works in Western Montana.

She is grateful for the many humans, events, and materials that contributed to her conception of this book: Anne Boyer's *Handbook of Disappointed Fate*, Chris Kraus' *I Love Dick*, Dorothea Lasky's *Why I Am Sad*, Dan & Gayle (February), Hoa Nguyen's *Red Juice*, Highway Ice Plant (*Carpobrotus edulis*), SpaceX, Bernie Sanders, *The Relentless Picnic*, Ariana Reines' *Open Fifths*, Neil Young's *On the Beach*, The World (The Devil), and Twitter dot com.

This book is for Jay, the center of her world, who told her to go back and look at her notes. Thanks to Emily, Emily, Suzanne, Bex, Cassandra, Nick, Jordan, and Jon-Michael for reassuring her she wasn't insane.

Some of these poems were published by *Gramma Poetry*, *Pouch Magazine*, *The New York Tyrant*, and Monster House Press. Thanks to the editors of these journals for sharing these poems (all poems). Thanks especially to Carrie and Janaka for seeing and believing, again.